My Brother and Me

(From Illness to Miracles, Hopelessness to Hope)

Dedicated in loving memory to my brother,

David Walker Elkins

June 14,1968-February 27, 2015

Book Cover Artwork – Self Portrait of David Elkins he drew in 1995.

Acknowledgements

First and foremost, I thank God for never giving up on me and providing me with your forgiveness, mercy, and grace. I thank you for all the protection you've provided me over the years and for allowing me to start fresh. Acts 3:19-20(NLT)- Now repent of your sins and turn to God, so that your sins may be wiped away. Then times of refreshment will come from the presence of the Lord, and he will again send you Jesus, your appointed Messiah.

I am so thankful that you are a forgiving God.

Chris, my husband and partner in this thing called life, I thank you for your support and for your willingness to do what is right for our family. Thank you for holding me accountable in those moments when my faith was wavering. I especially thank you for opening your heart up and allowing Christ in. That decision has changed not only you, but our family for the better.

Mom and Dad, thank you for your endless support over the years and for being such an amazing example in caring for your family through all circumstances. It has carried over as I feel unconditional love for my own son who faces his own battle of autism. Thank you for allowing me to share our family and David's story with others.

 My sweet son Carter, they say that love needs no words, and that is true. In my 6 years of being your mom, you have shown me love in your own ways, through your sweet eyes and smile and your precious laugh. You have helped me to grow in faith, patience, understanding, and acceptance.

Contents:

Conclusion

Introduction

Growing up in a family with a member who battles disease can be tough. At times you feel sad, other times frightened or confused. Such an array of emotions that come with this. You still go about your lives as normal as possible. You still celebrate birthdays and holidays and give God thanks for allowing you to have one more. A strength seems to just come to you naturally when you start to feel emotionally drained because your loved one needs you to be there for them. I believe God provides us with this strength when we as humans don't physically have anything left. Isaiah 40:31(NLT)- But those who trust in the Lord will find new strength. They will soar high on wings like eagles. They will run and not grow weary. They will walk and not faint.

Over the years after my older brother David's kidneys failed, I got to see firsthand the affects that disease can have on a human body. In his earlier days of his kidney disease, though disabled, he still seemed to have a lot of energy to do things. As the years passed and his health continued to decline, I watched his energy level decrease and his body age extremely fast. My middle-aged brother seemed to have the body of a 90-year-old man. He was frail and walked hunched over towards the end of his life. After battling for so long in his earthly body, God would call him home to his eternal life. A life that everyone who believes in God will have. John 3:16(ESV)- For God so loved the world, that he gave his only son, that whoever believes in him should not perish but have eternal life.

 One can only imagine what it is truly like in that eternal place called Heaven. I find peace knowing that my brother is there experiencing all the wonders and joy that the Lord provides. He no longer struggles with physical and emotional pain but has perfect peace.

Revelation 7:16-17(NLT)- They will never again be hungry or thirsty; they will never be scorched by the heat of the sun. For the Lamb on the throne will be their Shepard. He will lead them to springs of life-giving water. And God will wipe every tear from their eyes.

The Start to David's Battle

It was October 1991 about a month before my 12th birthday. I was in the 5th grade without a care in the world. I was all about playing with my friends and riding my bike all over our small town. It was probably during my New Kids on the Block and garbage pail kids' phase. I was in class one day and my mom showed up to get me early. I briefly remember her talking to my teacher and telling her that my oldest brother David had been taken by helicopter to the hospital. My young brain didn't quite grasp that being flown in a helicopter meant you were in danger of dying. I remember thinking, "David gets to fly in a helicopter, cool!" I soon would start to realize that a flight in a helicopter to the hospital was in fact, not a cool thing.

David had been sick recently with headaches and flu-like symptoms and had went to see our family doctor who put him on medication to treat his symptoms. He was living at my grandmother's house at the time. My grandma noticed one day that David seemed to be hallucinating. He was sitting at the dining room table smoking an unlit cigarette and pretending to deal a deck of cards.

What no one knew at the time was that David's kidneys had failed and his body was filling up with fluid, which was affecting his brain, causing the hallucinations. My grandmother knew something wasn't right and she called an ambulance. The ambulance came and took David to the local hospital where he was struggling to breathe. After assessing him, they called my mom at work and told her she needed to get to Borgess hospital in Kalamazoo, Michigan where they were having him life flighted to. My mom took me to a neighborhood friend's home and her and my dad went to Borgess hospital where they prepared my parents for the worse. My brother who had recently turned 22 years old a few months before was now in the fight for his life and the doctors didn't expect him to survive while in surgery. He made it through the surgery and was diagnosed with the rare kidney disease Glomerulonephritis. He was in intensive care for a while, and I remember not understanding why my mom wasn't allowing me to go with her to see him. I remember going a few blocks down the road to this older ladies' house that I knew and hiding under her porch area as I was upset and didn't understand why I couldn't see my brother. After my mom located me, she decided to allow me to go to Kalamazoo with her. We walked into David's room and surprisingly they had him sitting up in bed and he was able to talk to us. He still had quite a few tubes. I remember the feeding tube that was going from his nose down into his stomach, but he was coherent, and he was alive. The Lord had spared my brother and given us more time with him. Psalm 23:4(ESV)- Even though I walk through the valley of the shadow of death, I will fear no evil, for you are with me; your rod and your staff, they comfort me.

 Our family soon learned what a dialysis machine was. Due to there not being a dialysis center in our area yet, my mom had to drive David over an hour away to Kalamazoo for dialysis treatments 3 times a week. Once school was out for winter, spring, and summer breaks, I was able to ride along and keep my mom and brother company during his 4-hour long treatments. I was kind of amazed at the tubes that took my brother's blood, cleaned it, and returned it to his body. This machine was helping my brother to stay alive. With his kidneys not functioning, my brother had to have some adjustments with his diet and watch his fluid and salt intake. I can remember Mrs. Dash seasoning always being on the table because it was salt-free. At times, David's blood pressure would drastically drop, and we would have to quickly make him some beef broth to increase his salt-intake bringing his blood pressure back up before he had a chance to pass out on us. It was an adjustment for not only him, but for our whole family. David at age 22 was now disabled and moved back home. This was the start of a very long journey ahead, a journey filled with prayers for healing. Romans 8:26-27(NLT)- And the Holy Spirit helps us in our weakness. For example, we don't know what God wants us to pray for. But the Holy Spirit prays for us with groanings that cannot be expressed in words. And the Father who knows all hearts knows what the Spirit is saying, for the Spirit pleads for us believers in harmony with God's own will.

Summer in the South

 Father's Day weekend of 1992, my grandparents from Missouri had been to Michigan to visit us. I wanted to go back to Missouri with them for what I was thinking could be a summer vacation. My mom was hesitant at first but knowing that she had her hands full with caring for my brother, she agreed to let me go for the summer. I was so excited as I packed my suitcase bringing along the only 1 dress I owned for church, as I was very much a tomboy at that time with my shorts and ball cap. I grabbed my little bit of allowance that I had saved up in hopes of going swimming at the public pool down the road from my grandparent's home. We said our goodbyes and hopped into grandpa's van and headed for the south.

 My grandfather was a preacher for the Church of God of Prophecy, and I would soon learn just how strict my grandparents really were. My mom used to take us to church when I was small but I remember being scared and shy and not wanting to go to Sunday school so she would allow me to stay with her during the sermon where I'd color and eat a baggie of dry cheerios. My siblings would whine about having to go to church and once my mom started working on weekends we stopped going, so I hadn't had a lot of time in church up to this point. After getting to Missouri, my grandma went to some yard sales and bought me a handful of dresses as I would be in church while I was there. My grandpa preached at a very small church with only a few people in attendance. We were there on Wednesday evening, Friday evening, Sunday morning, and Sunday evening. One of the ladies there taught me how to play the tambourine which I enjoyed because I always loved music. After church, my grandparents would have their members over for meals and I would be shooed off to wash the dishes from their social time.

I soon realized that there wasn't much for a 12-year-old to do in Dexter, Missouri. There was a boy around my age that lived across the street from my grandparents and one day he came over and invited me to go to that public pool I was hoping to go to. My grandma quickly told me no. While talking to my mom later, she told me that my grandparents didn't believe in boys and girls swimming together. I was of course bummed that I never got to go to that swimming pool that I so desired to swim in.

Not to long after that, the house across the street burned down and that family moved. I would watch television, and not having cable, only a few channels came in. After watching a game show, a soap opera came on and my grandfather came unglued, lecturing me about watching a soap opera and how that wasn't allowed. I missed my friends and family and wished I had stayed home that summer. When I would talk to my mom on the phone, I would always ask, "how long before you can come and get me?" I would have to tough it out until the end of summer. I tried to make the most of it and would help my grandma pick and snap the green beans from her garden and on occasion we would go to the flea market and look at antiques. Grandma's sister, my "Aunt Nene" lived next door and I would go watch television with her a lot. One evening while I was watching the music awards with my grandma, she told me "you know, if you keep listening to this rock and roll music, you're going to go to hell." I couldn't believe she said that, but like I said, they were very strict and after my summer there, I no longer desired to go back or to go to church as I figured I would be judged for everything that I did.

 Now that I'm older, I sometimes wish that I would have grown up more in church, one that practiced more Christianity and acceptance as opposed to just religion and rules, but all things happen for a reason and I wasn't in a place of spiritual maturity. I would have a lot of life changes to go through in the future before finally getting to that place in my walk with Christ. 1 Peter 2:2-3(NLT)- Like newborn babies, you must crave pure Spiritual milk so that you will grow into a full experience of salvation. Cry out for this nourishment, now that you have had a taste of the Lord's kindness.

Transplant and A New Start

 After getting back to Michigan, I remember my mom taking me shopping for some back-to-school clothing. I picked out a couple pairs of stretch pants and a couple t-shirts. I can remember her apologizing for not being able to afford to do more that year for school clothes, but even at 12 years old, I was understanding and was happy with what I got. Maybe that trip to my grandparents' house did do me some good after all. It made me thankful for what I had. 1 Thessalonians 5:18 (ESV)- Give thanks in all circumstances; for this is the will of God in Christ Jesus for you.

 I was now a 6th grader and back with my friends. My mom was busy caring for my brother as well as the rest of our family. My dad, a hardworking man would come home around 4:00p.m. after a long day in the factory he worked at and my mom would always have our dinner ready when he got home. I think everyone's favorite meal has always been her homemade chicken and dumplings. I've never had any that has tasted as good as hers.

 Time continued to pass, and my brother and the family continued to adjust to this new lifestyle. David would get sick quite often, but when he felt well enough, he would stay in his room and work on his artwork. He was always such a talent when it came to art, even our local police department hired him to design their patch for them. He painted amazing Vincent Van Gogh pieces that were just as good as the originals and drew amazing sketches. He even knew how to crochet. One year he crocheted me the cutest stuffed mouse for Christmas. I still have it to this day.

 A little more time passed, and David's turn came up on the transplant list and there was a match so David would be getting a new kidney. We were all so excited that he would hopefully have a fresh and healthy start. David went through the surgery and received his new kidney in 1992. It was a long process. There was a nurse that would come to our home and give David treatments that were anti-rejection treatments to hopefully help his body to adjust to the new kidney and not reject it. I remember him lying there on a bed that was made for him downstairs with an I.V. in his arm. I remember freaking out and running to hide in the other room as he vomited in a bucket. Puke has always freaked me out. Eventually David's body started to adjust. He had a few scares, one which took place at the start of my birthday slumber party. My parents had to rush him to the hospital. My older cousin was there for my birthday and she offered to stay so that my friends didn't have to go home. We had our fun with movies and popcorn and probably some mischief as well as I was a little on the prankster side. I wasn't voted class clown for nothing. David was also a jokester; I think it runs in the family.

David slowly started to get better and was soon off the anti-rejection treatments. Things were looking up for him. He got enrolled into our local college and started taking classes focusing on art. I was amazed as he shared with me these pieces that he had sketched. They all looked so life like. Anytime a friend would come over I would ask him to show his artbook to them. I was so proud of my big brother and his talent and I wanted to show him off. During this time, David re-connected with an old girlfriend from high school who I believe he loved very much. She lived in Georgia making it a long-distance relationship. She flew him out to see her and took him to an Atlanta Braves game. David always loved baseball, especially the Chicago Cubs. I remember him sketching a picture of her, so I knew he loved her. Colossians 3:14 (ESV)- And above all these put on love, which binds everything together in perfect harmony.

Back to Dialysis

 David had his new routine in life down as he went to class and would go spend time with my uncles who were around his age quite often. My grandma had 13 children so some of them were close in age to my brother who was my parents first born. It was common back then to get married and have children before the age of 20. David was more like a brother to them instead of a nephew. My brother even moved in with them as roommates at one time. His life seemed to have turned around.

 It was 1996, almost 4 years after David received his kidney, and David became sick, and it was determined that his body had rejected the new kidney. They took him into surgery and removed the kidney and placed a shunt into his arm where he would be hooked up to dialysis through. Life had now shifted back to dialysis treatments 3 times a week. David dropped out of college and the relationship with his high school girlfriend stopped.

I can't even imagine what a hard blow that must have been for him, but my brother was a fighter and had a will to live. At one point, he even took some classes and received a diploma from the National Kidney Foundation of Michigan to be a trained peer counselor for others who were starting their journey with dialysis. Despite his own health struggles, he was willing to help others. Galatians 6:2(NLT)- Share each other's burdens, and in this way obey the law of Christ.

By now there had been a dialysis center built in our area so that took the burden of such a long drive off my mom as she could take him and drop him off and come get him when he was done. At one point, David saved up enough money and bought himself a small car. On the days that he felt well enough, he would drive himself around. That little white car was his source of freedom.

Over the years David continued his treatments and spent time doing artwork. At one point he invested in a tattoo kit and gave tattoos to my sister and my uncle. He even gave himself a tattoo of a little green frog on his upper leg. I wanted one but I was too young, and he hadn't ordered anymore needles so the tattoo art was short lived. Sometimes he would get hired to do artwork jobs sketching photographs of people or painting murals in my cousin's bedrooms. That kept him going and gave him some independence. When he wasn't in his room doing art or out fishing, we would play Skip Bo, UNO, and Yahtzee and we would watch movies together. He introduced me to the comedian Adam Sandler, and we sat and memorized every word of the movie Billy Madison and would laugh and joke and eat candy. He always had those maple nut goodies and Boston baked beans candy and would share with me as I have a major sweet tooth too. I cherished those times we spent together.

 The years of dialysis and the medications that David was on continued to take a toll on his body. It seemed like as a middle-aged man, his long dark brown hair seemed to turn pure white overnight making him look so much older than he was. He always resembled my mom's side of the family the most. The Cherokee Indian genes were strong and when he would leave his hair down, he almost looked like a full-blooded Indian. I'm sure he embraced that look because he was into collecting Indians, wolves, and dream catchers. He was in to collecting a lot of things. He had thousands of comic books he had collected over the years. I remember going to comic book shops with him and he'd get excited over lots of finds. He also started collecting brass items. All these things were his treasures, and he had each one displayed throughout his bedroom where he'd sit rocking out to his classic rock CDs. I think this is where I developed an interest in the older rock music. I love me some Journey and REO Speedwagon. When I hear the 70's and 80's rock, I can't help but think of my big brother. I looked up to him and admired his strength as he continued to jump each hurdle that was placed in his way. Hebrews 12:1(ESV)- Therefore, since we are surrounded by so great a cloud of witnesses, let us also lay aside every weight, and sin which clings so closely, and let us run with endurance the race that is set before us.

The Missing Piece

 I soon graduated high school and David gifted me with a screen print photograph of me he made, placed in a nice sturdy frame. He never had a lot of money as he had to live on disability, but he didn't let that stop him from giving thoughtful gifts to his family. All the hand made things are the most precious items that we could have received from him.

 After school I started working full-time and moved with a close friend into our first apartment, so I didn't always see David daily, but occasionally he'd come over for a change of scenery and visit with me. He was in and out of the hospital at times. I remember him having pneumonia and he had to have a few surgeries on the shunt that was implanted in his arm, as on occasion, it would stop working. Sometimes they'd take a little to much fluid off him at dialysis making him feel weak and sick. I don't know how he did it, but he did. He kept going and never tried to give up.

After a few years of living on my own, life circumstances brought me back to my parent's home. I was working full-time at the nursing home down the road from my parent's house as a cook and focusing on music the rest of the time. I would sing for our local cherry festival each 4th of July and go out to karaoke at the bars quite often. My mom's sunporch was my "practice space". The year of 2002 I started taking private vocal lessons. This amazing lady that was teaching me, had me learning classical songs to help open me up more. I was big into country music at the time, so we would work on that as well. It was around this time that I discovered that David liked more than classic rock. We would rock out to some Randy Travis together. He even started singing some country tunes on my karaoke machine.

It was 2004 and I came home from work and noticed there was a message on the machine. My mom was up at the hospital with David who was having another surgery on the shunt in his arm. I listened to the message and it was my aunt delivering the message that my grandma, who had been in the hospital, had passed away. My heart raced as I knew I had to contact my mom at the hospital. It broke my heart to deliver the news that her mom had passed. The visitation and funeral came and David, just getting out of the hospital, was to weak to go. I know that had to have broken his heart. He was always close to our grandma.

 A short amount of time after my grandma passed and after a relationship with my ex-fiancé had ended a couple years prior, I just felt like something was missing. When I was engaged, I was attending my exes catholic church with him. I had even gone to the series of classes and was baptized into the catholic faith. Soon after being baptized, my ex-fiancé broke up with me and broke my heart. Through that experience, I did a little songwriting and the song "All I Do Is Cry" was written, a song that would later go on my Nashville produced country album. I stopped attending the catholic church and sunk back into my party girl phase.

 Wanting to fill that space inside that was missing, I mentioned going to church to my dad and little did I know, he too was wanting to go to church. He mentioned a church that had been built just outside of town that looked nice and he'd like to try, so I made a deal with him, if he'd go to church with me, he could pick whatever church he wanted. That Sunday came and we attended Bright Star Tabernacle for the first time. Everyone was so nice and welcoming. The next Sunday we brought my mom along and this became our home church. This was a start to my own Christian faith journey. That missing piece was being filled by the only one who could fill it. Matthew 7:7-8(ESV)- Ask, and it will be given to you; seek, and you will find; knock, and it will be opened to you. For everyone who asks receives, and the one who seeks finds, and the one who knocks it will be opened.

The Album

 Soon after starting church, I was invited to start singing song specials at church. I mostly listened to country music at the time, so I didn't know a lot of the newer contemporary Christian or gospel music, so I started going to a local Christian bookstore where I could sample music and order CD's, so I soon started learning new music and singing in church. It felt great using my talent in church, but I still would go to karaoke most weeks and struggled to let go of the worldly desires that kept a hold on me. One evening I went to a new bar for karaoke, and I got up and belted out "I Drove All Night" by Celine Dion and the lady running karaoke was impressed with my vocal ability and she hooked me up with a contact she had. It was a music producer in Nashville Tennessee. I planned and a close friend traveled down to Tennessee with me to meet him. He was happy with my vocal ability as well and wanted to do an album with me. I soon learned how much it costs and let's just say, not cheap by any means, but I had big hopes for my dream of becoming the next country superstar and I knew the opportunity was hard to come by, so I opened 3 credit cards and went through the process of creating an album and becoming a "Nashville Recording Artist." After several months the album was complete, I had a website, a myspace page, and an album and mp3s for sale over the internet. Of course, I gave my family copies first. David had his proudly displayed along with his cd collection hanging on his wall.

 I had the cd tracks for my songs, so I was able to perform them at several festivals around the area to try and get myself out there more. At one point, I thought maybe I could do something to help a cause that was now close and personal to our family, so I contacted the National Kidney Foundation of Michigan and offered to do a fundraiser for them. There were some generous sisters that owned a reception hall and agreed to team up with me. I went and had tickets printed to sell, they would keep a certain amount to cover the food costs and the rest would go to my cause. I also was able to get certain companies to donate items for a silent auction. I put on a performance and sold CD's. It turned out pretty good and I was able to send them the funds that were raised. In return, they invited me to sing that spring at their kidney walk event. I always hoped that I made my big brother proud.

 At one karaoke contest I met a fellow contestant that I soon became close friends with. She had recorded an album with the same producer in the past and had the same music dreams, so we hit it off from the start. We soon started planning for a move together to Nashville, TN. We started singing together and living the sinful nightlife together most weekends. I'm now ashamed of how I would binge drink on Friday night and turn around and sing in God's house on Sunday morning. I was defiantly caught up in the pleasures of worldly things. If only I had followed this passage: Romans 12:2(NLT)- Don't copy the behavior and customs of this world, but let God transform you into a new person by changing the way you think. Then you will learn to know God's will for you, which is good and pleasing and perfect.

The Heart Attack

 March 3, 2008 started out a normal day. I had the day off work and was sitting at the kitchen table with my mom after having lunch. David had been out picking up his prescriptions at the drug store. He soon came flying in the door and ran straight to the bathroom. We both just assumed he had to throw up because that happened to him a lot. After a few minutes the bathroom door opened, and he was on his hands and knees yelling that he couldn't breathe. Right away I noticed that his skin color had a grayish tint, and this was now a serious emergency. Thankfully the phone was right there next to me, so without hesitation I grabbed it and called 911. I had to step outside the door to hear the operator between David's screams and my mom's. After a few minutes which felt like forever, a police officer arrived. At this point David had shallow breathing and was vomiting but still had a pulse. Soon the paramedics arrived, they couldn't get a pulse at this point. I held on to my mom and stayed out of their way as they shocked my brother's chest several times. They finally managed to get a pulse and got him loaded into the ambulance. We called my dad, sister, and other brother so they could meet us at the emergency room. I insisted on driving us there. I did not want my mom driving after what we'd just witnessed. We arrived at the emergency room and were taken into the trauma room where David was lying there on a ventilator, hooked up to so many tubes and machines. The sight was defiantly horrific. Once they had him stable enough, he was moved to the critical care unit. He had had a heart attack and one of his lungs had collapsed. He was placed in a drug induced coma and they were unsure of how much brain activity he had. Only time and a series of tests would tell.

 After about a week the doctors tried to slowly take David out of the coma to see how he'd do. He kicked and tried to pull the tubes out, so they had to put restraints on his wrists and put him back in the coma. I remember at one point when my mom and I were alone in the elevator getting ready to head home for the night, she broke down. I remember her saying that it felt crewel him being on those machines and suffering. She said she almost felt like telling them to unhook him and let him go. I'm so glad she didn't. There were prayers going up all over. I asked for prayers on my artist page on myspace and we had our church praying over him. Our pastor even came to the hospital and prayed over him. It was comforting knowing that so many people were praying. Matthew 18:20(ESV)- For where two or three are gathered in my name, there am I among them.

 One evening when we were all up at the hospital in the CCU waiting room, a family came in and they were in tears and sobbing. I think all our hearts sank as we knew that those tears meant that their loved one didn't make it. We quickly left the waiting room to give them some privacy. I think we were all terrified that we'd have to make that same decision soon. Week 1 soon turned into week 2. At one point, David's best friend who was a doctor, came to visit. He said with David being younger he had a better chance at surviving which made me feel more at ease. The doctors did their tests and continued to monitor progress. They were able to gradually lower the oxygen levels on the ventilator and soon brought David out of the coma. He had to continue to wear the restraints because he was bound and determined to pull that vent tube out. The doctor said he was going to remove the tube one day, and then he changed his mind. On this day, I had gone back to work since David was improving. I called my mom on my lunch break to check in and David still had his brain function because he knew that the doctor had said he was going to remove the tube but then changed his mind. David had wiggled himself down far enough in the bed to reach the tube with his restrained wrists and grabbed and pulled the tube out himself. Lucky for him, he was able to breathe by himself again. I went to the hospital after I got off work and there was my big brother, sitting up in bed talking with a raspy voice. I remember feeling such a relief, knowing he was recovering. After a few days, David was moved to a regular room. Soon after that, he was released to come home.

 My mom had set up a bed downstairs for David until he had enough strength to climb the stairs to his bedroom. The morning after he came home, David shared with me a vision he had that evening. He said he had woken up in the middle of the night and in the doorway of my parent's bedroom, he saw an angel. He described it as a glowing figure with wings that had its face turned away from him and as it started to turn its face towards him, it vanished. I immediately got chills hearing this. My mom thought he was probably seeing things because of all the medications he was on but I'm choosing to believe that he saw an angel that night. Psalm 34:7(NLT)- For the angel of the Lord is a guard; he surrounds and defends all who fear him. A couple days later it was Easter Sunday and given that David had just been given another miracle of being alive, he desired to go with the family to church that Sunday. We all arrived at church, but soon my mom had to take David home as his blood pressure started to drop. He pushed himself a little to hard and his body wasn't quite healed enough yet.

 A few months passed and David was back to his normal routine of going to dialysis and spending a lot of time in his bedroom. He wasn't doing much artwork anymore because over the years he had developed a lot of arthritis and was normally in pain. One evening when getting home from dialysis, he was in his room and he yelled out. I went to check on him and asked if he needed an ambulance and he said yes. I called 911 again and the paramedics took him to the hospital, and he was put on a ventilator again and this time he had a stroke on both sides of his brain. This time around it wasn't as long of a hospital stay. He was only on the ventilator for a day and then in a regular room and soon released. Once again, I was amazed at how he continued to pull out of these life-threatening situations. God had continued to perform miracles on my brother, that alone should have been proof enough that God is real, and He is alive. Matthew 19:26(ESV)- But Jesus looked at them and said, "with man this is impossible, but with God all things are possible."

We Prayed

 Summer of 2008 I spent performing at local festivals and singing song specials at church while saving money and preparing to move to Nashville. I made a trip to Nashville with the friend I was singing with and we got our apartment locked in while there. After coming back home to Michigan, I had this desire in my heart to write a song based on the event that happened to my brother on March 3rd. I sat with my paper and pen and a melody in my head and it just flowed out. Only God could have placed that there to come out so easily. Philippians 2:13(NLT)- For God is working in you, giving you the desire and the power to do what pleases him. I took this song to my vocal teacher and she arranged music to go with it. As a woman who was blind, she certainly did not let that keep her from doing amazing things. I was always in awe of her and her husband's talents. Both legally blind but incredible talents and teachers. I had been taking guitar lessons with her husband for a couple years and thanks to him, I can play a little now. Soon after my teacher arranged music for me and put it on a track, I was able to get a copywrite on it and able to go to a recording studio and record it along with a few of the tracks that I sang to in church, and it became my Christian demo. The song was called We Prayed.

We Prayed

Verse 1: As we heard the sirens drive away, me and momma knew life would never be the same. As we wondered what would happen next, we knew the Lord would be there every step.
Chorus 1: And we cried, and we prayed, and we knew the Lord would be there by our side. And with him there in our lives, everything would be alright, and we prayed, oh how we prayed.
Verse 2: As we walked into the CCU, my brother lye there fighting for his life. The days and hours and minutes passed, we wondered just how long that this would last.
Repeat Chorus 1: And we cried, and we prayed, and we knew the Lord would be there by our side. And with him there in our lives, everything would be alright, and we prayed, oh how we prayed.
Bridge: Momma called me on the phone, said your brothers sitting here, and he's ready to come home.
Chorus 2: And we cried, and we prayed, and we

knew the Lord had been there by our side. And he was there, in our lives, and now everything was alright. And we prayed, oh how we prayed, yeah, we prayed, oh how we prayed, yeah, we prayed.

 I remember David telling me that he had played "We Prayed" for the medic one driver who was now transporting him to and from dialysis treatments, and that it made her cry. I felt like he was proud of me and what little sister doesn't want their older siblings to be proud of her?

 August 25, 2008 came, and it was moving day. I packed my car as full as possible, and the rest had been placed in a rental truck along with my friend's belongings. I said my goodbyes to the family and headed for Nashville, TN. I remember feeling a little sad leaving my hometown, the only place I'd ever known, but also feeling a sense of freedom as I was going off to start a new life in a big city. Deuteronomy 31:6(ESV)- Be strong and courageous. Do not fear or be in dread of them, for it is the Lord your God who goes with you. He will not leave you or forsake you.

Nashville

We arrived in Nashville just in the nick of time to get the keys to our new home before the apartment office closed and started unloading our belongings. It was a late night that evening before being able to rest. A few days after moving in, our hallway started to flood as my friend was taking a shower. It turned out that a pipe in the wall had busted so we were given a different apartment, so we basically moved twice. Talk about a bit of a rocky start. We settled in and started looking for jobs as we had only saved up enough to survive a couple months of being unemployed. We used MapQuest maps to get us around at first because we had no clue where we were going. I have to say I was overwhelmed with the crazy fast driving and all the lanes of traffic after coming from a small farmer community without even a stoplight. I had to learn the city way of driving fast if I didn't want to get run over. While looking for jobs we also found a small lounge where we could hang out and sing karaoke at, that was close to home. As I mentioned before, I was caught up in the pleasures of living the "night life." Why I desired something that often made me sick, I'm not so sure. But even in those days, God continued to watch over me and kept me safe from harm and never gave up on me, just like it says in the parable of the lost sheep. Matthew 18:12-13(NLT)- "If a man has a hundred sheep and one of them wanders away, what will he do? Won't he leave the ninety-nine others on the hills and go out to search for the one that is lost? And if he finds it, I tell you the truth, he will rejoice over it more than over the ninety-nine that didn't wander away!

Less than 2 months after moving, I landed a cooking job at one of the hospitals close to downtown. It seemed to start off ok but after a period, I was being treated poorly by certain employees including one of the supervisors because of my skin color. You see, I was one of only a few white people in that department. I always tried to treat people fairly and with respect and I was always a hard worker, giving it my all and helping others with their workload if I finished early, so all I could see was I was treated this way because of my skin color. Prejudice isn't just with one race and I feel for those who are victims of it because I was able to be in their shoes for a moment. I remember one lady trying to sabotage me by telling the boss man that I had thrown away an entire pan of food which I did not do. He knew I was being treated differently but he simply brushed it under the rug. The hate from the one supervisor was obvious. I would say good morning and she would put her nose in the air at me. A co-worker even overheard her say one time "I don't know why anyone would want to help that white broad." This woman was supposed to be a leader in our department. Well eventually she went on a medical leave and ended up losing her position, so that took care of that. Colossians 3:25(NLT)- But if you do what is wrong, you will be paid back for the wrong you have done. For God has no favorites.

I stuck it out at my job because they were paying me a decent wage and I had good health insurance and well, I had rent and necessities to pay. I ended up working there a little over 3 years and put myself through a dental assistant program during that time. My idea was to get into a dental office so I'd have good hours and weekends off for music and so I could escape the job that I dreaded. I did great during the classroom portion and maintained a 4.0 grade average and perfect attendance. Once I finished that and started going to work interviews and was practicing hands on, I quickly realized this was not my calling and I felt very uncomfortable trying to do it, so I didn't follow through with this as a career. I continued to work hard at my hospital job until a new door opened. 2 Chronicles 15:7(NLT)- But as for you, be strong and courageous, for your work will be rewarded.

Love, Marriage, and Music

 The end of May 2009 I met my now husband Chris at that local lounge I would hang out at. He was there playing pool quite often and one night we decided to hang out. Of course, the drinks were flowing but I remember thinking he's cute and seems like he's got a silly personality which I tend to like as I've always been a bit on the goofy side. After hanging out at the bar a couple times, we went out on a couple dates and started spending more time together and became a couple. A couple months into our relationship, Chris had started showing his cocky hot-tempered side which I was certainly not digging. I ended up breaking up with him, I wanted no part of feuding and not feeling valued by someone who supposedly cared about me. I still would run into him at that lounge but kept my distance at first. A few months passed and it was my 30th birthday. I, of course, went to my normal hangout and Chris was there. I knew he was sorry for not treating me right and I found it in my heart that night to show forgiveness towards him and we started a relationship again. Ephesians 4:32(ESV)- Be kind to one another, tenderhearted, forgiving one another, as God in Christ forgave you.

 Like all couples, we still had our disagreements and feuds from time to time but we pushed past it the best we could. I brought Chris home to meet my family and was impressed with how well they seemed to like him, especially my mom who never seemed to approve of any of my past boyfriends. David found out that Chris collected marvel movies, so they had a little something in common as David loved his comic books. He even had the figurines of comic book characters on a shelf hanging on his bedroom wall. Seeing how much they approved of him was a sign for me and 2 years later we were married. Our wedding day came on September 3, 2011 over Labor Day weekend. We were married in Nashville so that required our family to travel to us this time. Due to David's health, he was unable to come.

 I had recently joined up with my friend and some local Nashville musicians and after a handful of rehearsals we started playing as a cover band at local bars and venues around the outskirts of Nashville. Sometimes we'd play to a packed house, other times to mostly empty chairs. You just never knew whether you'd have a crowd or not, but it was always so exciting when it was a big energetic crowd. We even played at a couple biker rallies. Those were interesting to say the least. I was now working in a pre-school center as my day job, so I had my weekends free for performing and I was living it up, singing every weekend.

A New Life

 Over the next few years, I continued to perform with the band and worked in preschool. We would try and make a trip home to Michigan at least once a year to see my family. Normally around Thanksgiving is when we'd go, and we'd take care of Christmas gifts at that time too. I would notice each year that David seemed to decline more in his health. He was getting around slowly and like I mentioned before, he looked so much older than he was. His arthritis had gotten worse, and he had developed COPD (Chronic Obstructive Pulmonary Disease). It was obvious that he was in a lot of pain most days, but he kept on going because he had a will to live. He was in and out of the hospital still with bouts of pneumonia or problems with the shunt in his arm, each time weakening in his strength. It was sad to see him in that condition. I think a part of me felt guilty for leaving home, but I felt like I needed my own life somewhere else at the same time.

January 2014 came, and I started a normal weekday routine of going to work. After work I stopped at the tanning salon I had been going to and while lying in the tanning bed I felt a weird fluttering sensation in my stomach. I was like hmm that's weird. I also remembered that Chris and I hadn't been doing anything to prevent us from getting pregnant either. We'd been married over 2 years now, so we felt like we were ready to start a family. After leaving the salon, I stopped at the store on the way home and picked up a pregnancy test. I had taken a few before and they always came up negative, so I was expecting this one to read the same. Well, I was wrong, this one was clearly positive. I took the 2nd test to be sure and yes it was also positive. We were living in the apartment community where Chris worked, so I called him and asked him to come home for a few minutes. He came home and looked at the test and looked like a deer in the headlights at first, but then was happy and excited after the shock wore off. Other than a little queasy feeling from the smell of coffee of all things, and a little tired, my pregnancy was smooth for most of it. I continued performing every weekend throughout my pregnancy, baby bump and all. I had the typical routine checkups and was taking the expensive doctor prescribed pre-natal vitamins. Life was just moving along smoothly.

While my brother's quality of life was taking another turn for the worse, a new life was growing inside of me.

 A couple of months before going home to Michigan for my baby shower, my sister called as I was walking in from a doctor's appointment. She normally didn't call a lot, so my gut instinct told me something was wrong before I answered the phone. David who was now on oxygen full-time, had another episode. She didn't call me until he had been stabilized. They had called for the family to come in as he was not waking up this time around. Our pastor went in and prayed over him and then he woke up. That's just more proof that God's word is alive. James 5:14(NLT)- Are any of you sick? You should call for the elders of the church to come and pray over you, anointing you with oil in the name of the Lord. I told you David was a fighter. Yet again he survived when most others would not have. It's amazing the miracles God can perform.

 At this point, David's health had deteriorated to the point that he was unable to properly take care of himself and my parents who are aging and have health problems of their own were unable to provide him the care he needed. I know it had to be a devastating decision, one that probably haunted them, but David upon being discharged from the hospital, was placed in a nursing home. I believe that God stayed close by him through this. Joshua 1:9 (NLT)- This is my command- be strong and courageous! Do not be afraid or discouraged. For the Lord your God is with you wherever you go.

The New Baby

 June 2014, I came home for my baby shower. It was the same weekend as David's birthday. We went to visit him at the nursing home and my mom made his favorite cherry chip cake. We used the community dining room and had a little birthday party for him. He looked so sad. After years of declining health, the depression was starting to take a toll now, but he opened his gifts and we visited for a while. I made sure to go and visit him again before leaving to go back to Nashville.

 September 10th, I went in for my O.B. visit. Our son's due date was predicted for September 23rd but considering how big I was as well as the pain I was now in with my back, that I'd already had problems with for a few years, my doctor set a date for me to be induced on the 17th and did something to hopefully move things along. I remember thinking, please just don't let him be born on September 11th. I want his birthday to not be on a day that is remembered for tragedy. The whole day of September 11th I felt weird. I was having a lot of pain in my back and now it felt like my right leg kept coming out of the socket. I powered through my workday and was planning on starting my maternity leave on that Monday. Friday September 12th around 1:00am I woke up to go use the bathroom. It was dark as I normally don't turn the lights on in the middle of the night, so I couldn't see much. After using the rest room, I started to get up and was like, am I still peeing? So, I sat back down and then it clicked, oh that's my water breaking. I yelled for Chris to wake up. He was in such a panic it was kind of cute. I told him to relax and take the dog out to potty and let me get dressed and then we we'd go to the hospital. I wasn't in much pain yet and didn't notice the contractions. I believe Chris was speeding the entire way to the hospital. He probably watched to many shows in the past and was worried about a car birth. We got to the hospital and got checked in and was there for a little while before I started feeling uncomfortable. Once the pains in my lower back started, I was given an epidural and a catheter. My legs were so numb that I couldn't physically move them. I was feeling no pain at the time. It was around 4:00pm before I was finally dilated to 10 cm and ready to push. Once we got to the point of our baby getting close to coming out, I had forgotten about that epidural and it was the most horrific pain I'd ever felt. Finally, at 5:11pm on September 12, 2014 our son Carter John entered the world. He was the cutest, chunkiest 9lb baby boy I'd ever laid eyes on. Psalm 127:3(NLT)- Children are a gift from the Lord; they are a reward from him.

 We settled into our apartment with our new addition and looked forward to introducing our pride and joy to our family and friends. My sister and her family came to visit us when Carter was 1 month old, so they were the first from my side of the family to meet him. At 2 months old we were able to make a trip home to Michigan for Thanksgiving weekend so the rest of the family could meet Carter. Chris went with my dad to pick up David from the assisted living home where he was now staying after being discharged from the nursing home. He walked in the house with a little assistance dragging his oxygen along. He was so skinny and frail. His once long thick hair was now very thin and stringy, he was extremely pail and walked hunched over. I remember thinking he looked like a walking corpse. I sat next to him on the couch with Carter so he could get a glimpse of his new nephew. I offered to let him hold him, but he chose not to. I think being as weak as he was, he was probably afraid he'd drop him. His face looked so sad, and it broke my heart seeing the state he was in. The brother who was always such a fighter, his quality of life was in a state of despair now. I choked back my feelings as I didn't want him to see me looking sad and I offered to make his plate of food. It was a short visit as David grew tired, so my dad took him back to his assisted living home. Psalm 73:26(NLT)- My health may fail, and my Spirit may grow weak, but God remains the strength of my heart; he is mine forever.

Life After Death

Friday February 27, 2015, I woke up to my alarm clock around 5:00am and was going to start getting ready for work. I went to the kitchen in our new house we had purchased a couple months before and started the coffee pot. My cell phone started ringing and my parent's phone number came up. Mom didn't normally call me at this time of day so before I answered, I braced myself because I knew from my gut instinct why she was calling. I answered and it was the news I was expecting. David had suffered another heart attack in the middle of the night but this time they were unable to bring him back. He fought for so long, but his body couldn't fight any longer, he was finally able to rest. At the age of 46, after living with dialysis treatments for 24 years, my brother no longer had to suffer. The average life expectancy on dialysis is said to be around 5-10 years but my brother far exceeded that number and was proof that while he was here on earth that God does work miracles.

Plans for his service were made and the outpouring of love from those around us was comforting. We grieved with sadness but rejoiced knowing he was in heaven in a new healthy body with no more pain or sickness. Revelation 21:4(NLT)- He will wipe every tear from their eyes, and there will be no more death or sorrow or crying or pain. All these things are gone forever.

My little family made the trip home to Michigan for David's funeral. Carter was now 5 months old, and he was a happy bouncy baby and brought joy to everyone during such a sad time. He was the best kind of distraction. My family chose to do an open casket during the visitation. David was dressed in a sweater that he had worn for his high school senior pictures with his Chicago cub's baseball hat placed on his head. He was representing his favorite team as he always had. During the service my sister spoke. I know it took a lot of strength for her to do that without breaking down. After the memorial, we headed to the cemetery where Chris was one of the pall bearers. I know it must have been hard for him as he had lost his younger brother tragically several years before, so I was proud of him for doing it. It was extremely cold outside for the graveside service with snow on the ground. After we left the cemetery, we gathered back at our church for food and fellowship. After that was over, we dug through old VHS tapes from when I was in high school. I used to play with my dad's camcorder and there were several clips of David doing silly skits on them as well as some where he was looking annoyed at me. Yes, I was the pesky little sister to my siblings. We sat there remembering the good times and got a good laugh out of those videos. The next day we said our goodbyes and headed home. That weekend after David's funeral, I noticed Chris reading a small new testament bible that a co-worker had given him. Chris had never been interested in anything relating to church in the past, so I feel like something happened with my brother's death and funeral that caused a relationship with Christ to start to emerge. It was the start of a new journey for our little family.

 I've at times seen people and had to do a second glance because they resembled my brother. I've seen some of David's looks in my son's face as well. One time I was taking pictures of clouds and a cloud resembled David's face and it looked like his little dog Arthur next to him. I take it as a sign that he's with God and happy. We miss him every day, especially during holidays, but he is always with us in our hearts. Revelation 14:13(NLT)- And I heard a voice from heaven saying, write this down: Blessed are those who die in the Lord from now on. Yes, says the Spirit, they are blessed indeed, for they will rest from their hard work; for their good deeds follow them!"

Conclusion

I'm not sure why my brother ended up with such a horrible sickness for so many years of his life. Why he didn't get to experience marriage and children and the typical things a healthy man would experience, but as it says in Romans 8:28, God causes everything to work together for good. I do know that in his amount of time here and through his illness, I got to see firsthand the amount of strength he had as he fought to stay alive another day. In his time here, I got to witness God performing miracle after miracle. Through his illness, it kept our family close, and it kept us aware of God's presence in our lives. Through my brother's death, I feel like that was a turning point in my husband's coming to God moment. Where one life was lost, another's life was found. Luke 15:10(NLT)- In the same way, there is joy in the presence of God's angels when even one sinner repents.

Life is truly better and more fulfilling with God at the center of it. If you don't have a relationship with Jesus Christ, please invite him into your heart. He is a loving and a forgiving God who shows us mercy and grace when we've done nothing and cannot do anything to deserve it. 1 John 1:9(NLT)- But if we confess our sins to him, he is faithful and just to forgive us our sins and to cleanse us from all wickedness. Please accept him today with this following prayer or one of your own. Our heavenly father accepts all prayers from the heart.

The Sinner's Prayer: (Billy Graham Version) Heavenly Father, I come to you in prayer asking for the forgiveness of my sins. I confess with my mouth and believe with my heart that Jesus is your son, and that he died on the cross at Calvary that I might be forgiven and have eternal life in the kingdom of heaven. Father, I believe that Jesus rose from the dead and I ask you right now to come into my life and be my personal Lord and Savior. I repent of my sins and will worship you all the days of my life. Because your word is truth, I confess with my mouth that I am born again and cleansed by the blood of Jesus. In Jesus Name, Amen.

Resources:

You Version Bible App.

www.biblestudytools.com

www.proverbs31.org

Google- Local churches in your area, Local Christian bookstores